JOANNA MURRAY-SMITH's plays have been produced in many languages, all over the world, including on the West End, Broadway and at the Royal National Theatre. Her plays include *Pennsylvania Avenue*, *Fury*, *Songs for Nobodies*, *Day One—A Hotel—Evening*, *The Gift*, *Rockabye*, *The Female of the Species*, *Ninety*, *Bombshells*, *Rapture*, *Nightfall*, *Redemption*, *Flame*, *Love Child*, *Atlanta*, *Honour* and *Angry Young Penguins*. She has also adapted *Hedda Gabler*, as well as Ingmar Bergman's *Scenes from a Marriage*, for Sir Trevor Nunn (London). Her three novels (published by Penguin/Viking) are *Truce*, *Judgement Rock* and *Sunnyside*. Her opera libretti include *Love in the Age of Therapy* and *The Divorce*. Joanna has also written many screenplays.

Kim Gyngell as William and Melinda Butel as Isabel in the 2008 MTC production. (Photo: Jeff Busby)

ninety

Joanna Murray-Smith

Currency Press, Sydney

CURRENCY PLAYS

First published in 2009
by Currency Press Pty Ltd,
PO Box 2287, Strawberry Hills, NSW, 2012, Australia
enquiries@currency.com.au
www.currency.com.au

Reprinted 2017, 2019.

NATIONAL LIBRARY OF AUSTRALIA CIP DATA

Author:	Murray-Smith, Joanna.
Title:	Ninety / Joanna Murray-Smith.
ISBN:	9780868198514 (pbk.)
Dewey Number:	A822.3

Typeset by Dean Nottle for Currency Press.

Printed by Fineline Print + Copy Services, St Peters, NSW.

Cover design by Laura McLean, Currency Press.

Cover shows Kim Gyngell as William and Melinda Butel as Isabel in the 2008 MTC production. (Photo: Jeff Busby)

Contents

For Raymond and the Pantheon.
And for Charlie.

Ninety was first produced by Melbourne Theatre Company at the Fairfax Theatre, Melbourne, on 22 August 2008 with the following cast:

ISABEL	Melinda Butel
WILLIAM	Kim Gyngell

Director, Simon Phillips
Set Designer, Andrew Bellchambers
Lighting Designer, Nick Schlieper

CHARACTERS

ISABEL, around forty

WILLIAM, five or six years older

SETTING

Isabel's work studio. It has as little or as much dressing as required, but the overall impression is of a room curated by an elegant eye. In the room is an easel with a very beautiful painting of a couple, done in the style of a Van Eyck and vaguely reminiscent of 'Mr and Mrs Arnolfini'. Hanging around the top of the easel is a watch.

THANKS

Ninety came into itself through the significant talents of Simon Phillips, Kym Gyngell, Melinda Butel and Rachel Griffiths. Thanks to all the staff of the Melbourne Theatre Company.

As always, I am indebted to Raymond Gill.

And particular thanks to Dr Joe Crameri, who wouldn't remember us.

As the play begins, ISABEL *is working at the easel with a tiny brush, small dabs interspersed with long periods of contemplation. The door opens and* WILLIAM *enters. The start of the play needs to show a playfulness built from history.*

WILLIAM: Your time starts now.

ISABEL: Latecomer.

WILLIAM: Scheduler.

ISABEL: I thought you might not [actually show]—

WILLIAM: Really?

ISABEL: Well.

WILLIAM: I said [I would]—

ISABEL: Yes, but—

WILLIAM: I said [I would]—

ISABEL: I know. [*Beat.*] But you said that last time.

WILLIAM: Ah. Last time.

ISABEL: And you didn't show.

WILLIAM: I was shooting.

ISABEL: No you weren't. I rang your agent. Max said there was a writers' strike in LA. *Nothing* was shooting. He said you were in Kenya. Some Abercrombie and Something luxury safari.

WILLIAM: That's what I mean. *Shooting*.

ISABEL: *Lions*? [*Beat.*] Even *I* know they're *protected*. Even *I* know all that went out with Hemingway.

WILLIAM: If you're very rich or famous they'll still let you sink an old gazelle or two while the World Wildlife Fund are taking tea.

ISABEL: *Cynic*.

WILLIAM: *Sentimentalist*.

ISABEL: It was good, actually. Last time.

WILLIAM: Good.

ISABEL: There is, as they say, something 'healing' in ceremony…

WILLIAM: Well.

ISABEL: It was lovely, actually. The park. The trees—

WILLIAM: 'In their burst of colour'—

ISABEL: In their burst of colour.

WILLIAM: I think we should let them go.

ISABEL: We should let them go?

WILLIAM: The dead. [*Beat.*] I don't believe in standing in a park and hearing *The Prophet* or *The Tibetan Book of the fucking Dead* and then going off to drink tea. Something about death sends tea consumption into a frenzy. I apologise.

ISABEL: It was lovely.

WILLIAM: Good. What did you do?

ISABEL: We went to the park. Marjorie read from… *The Tibetan Book of the fucking Dead.* Then we all came back to the house and… drank tea.

WILLIAM: Lovely.

ISABEL: I missed you.

WILLIAM: All right, so I didn't come. I'm busy. I have 'things on'. You may interpret this as self-importance and you may be right, but whatever, that's the way it is. I have *a life*. For what it's worth. I'm a citizen of the world of international travel *and I love it*. I apologise for my 'failure rate'. Anyway, enough about me. How are *you*?

She is about to respond when a small BlackBerry-type device/ phone starts beeping. He immediately pulls it out of his pocket, flips it open and reads the message, while she waits.

Huh! [*He starts laughing.*] Cheeky bastard! [*He starts tapping a message back.*] Stick that where it belongs! [*He looks up at* ISABEL.] Sorry! How *are* you?

ISABEL: Well, I'm—

The same device rings again. He flips it open.

WILLIAM: [*to the phone*] I'm busy! No. No, tell him if that stays, I walk. I walk! Don't talk to me about clauses. Don't fucking talk to me about clauses, speak English. I know. I know. I *know*. [*He snaps the device shut.*] Never leave me alone. It's horrific. My PA's brilliant, she's brilliant, but I'm her life. [*Ironically*] Sometimes I have to say, 'Back off, babe', you know what I'm saying?

ISABEL: Not really.

WILLIAM: The business.

ISABEL: Congratulations on being a Globe.

WILLIAM: You really don't get out much, do you? You don't *become* a Globe!

ISABEL: Oh.

WILLIAM: You *win* one. A Golden One. You make me sound like an *artichoke.*

ISABEL: Well, anyway, that was… something.

WILLIAM: A nice role. Great writing. Just happened to… tap into the zeitgeist.

ISABEL: You're very good, actually.

WILLIAM: Thank you, Isabel. Generous.

ISABEL: How is it, being famous?

WILLIAM: Oh, it's nice.

ISABEL: Good tables?

WILLIAM: *Great* tables. Reservations totally obsolescent.

ISABEL: The world of obsolescent reservations. Gosh.

WILLIAM: I've also got to the point where I can fly first and not eat every single thing that's offered to me. The *really* famous never, ever, *ever* eat. It's too *mortal.* They only drink bottled water.

ISABEL: I've read about it!

WILLIAM: All those truffle-tinged hors d'oeuvres and hot baked cookies four thousand miles above the Sahara are only for people for whom flying first is a special occurrence. The lovely hosties holding trays of superbly zapped morsels dip and sway, their tight little arses sashaying towards me in seat 1A. I say, 'No Thank You. Just some water, if you please, collected from that small bubbling spring in that newly discovered rainforest off the Amazon by very, very nice pygmies. And if you're all out of that, please don't worry your pretty little head about a damn thing. I'll just recline here, ever so slightly parched, and contemplate my fame.'

ISABEL: I suppose lots of women come your way now.

WILLIAM: Millions.

ISABEL: Do you bed all of them?

WILLIAM: Of course not! I'm not a *slut*! [*Beat.*] Just the blondes.

ISABEL: They mainly *would* be blondes, wouldn't they?

WILLIAM: Actually, I prefer brunettes, but I'm caught in a cliché.

ISABEL: When I think of all those nights you spent going to radical handicapped theatre troupes doing productions of seminal plays by obscure Finnish geniuses. In mime.

WILLIAM: Let me remind you: Income is the choreographer of ideology. [*He turns to the painting on the easel.*] This your latest, then?

ISABEL: Yes.

WILLIAM: Who are they?

ISABEL: Rock and Doris? We don't really know who they are. Probably a merchant and his wife.

WILLIAM: Rock and Doris, popular names in Antwerp in the sixteenth century, then?

ISABEL: They've been living with me for ten months, I had to call them something. It was found on a property in the Western District and dusted off by the beneficiaries. They want it restored, then they'll give it to Sothebys for auctioning next year.

WILLIAM: It looks like—

ISABEL: I know. But apparently not. There was some speculation it might have been an early study, but it's not Van Eyck. It's rather beautiful, don't you think? The supplication in his eyes—to what? God? Love?

WILLIAM: He might just be hungry. 'We've been sitting in front of this wanker for hours and has anyone offered us so much as a *pomme frite*?' [*Beat.*] Is it wonderful?

ISABEL: Is it wonderful to you?

WILLIAM: What do I know about wonderful?

ISABEL: I've stood in front of it for nearly a year, and still, it reveals something new almost every time I look at it.

WILLIAM: Nearly a year. Obsessive?

ISABEL: Patient. [*Beat.*] What astonishes me, is how little we've changed in five hundred years, we husbands and wives. There she is. Look at her. She's wondering where she becomes him, and where she is alone. Their faces were cloudier before. Layers and layers of varnish have come off. Hundreds of years of UV light, pollutants. Their gaze has been getting more distinct—

WILLIAM: You've been—

ISABEL: Bringing them back.

His BlackBerry goes off again.

WILLIAM: Oh fuck. [*He flips it open and reads.*] *Fuck me*! What's the point of delegating? [*Typing*] Tell. Them. No. Photo. Shoot. I don't care who they are. [*Pause. Typing as he speaks*] Who are they? [*He waits for a response. Typing and speaking*] Say yes, then!

ISABEL: What is that?

WILLIAM: It's like a BlackBerry, only much more expensive.

ISABEL: A BlackBerry?

WILLIAM: It's brilliant. And this one—the keyboard is enormous. Absolutely enormous. It's impossible to hit the wrong button.

ISABEL: But it's only two inches big.

WILLIAM: I have every fifteen minutes for the next month programmed into here. Can't live without it.

ISABEL: Can you turn it off?

WILLIAM: Technically it's turn-offable. But the concept makes me nervous.

She looks at him. He thinks. He turns it off and puts it aside.

ISABEL: [*surveying him*] Does someone take you shopping?

WILLIAM: Can you tell?

ISABEL: You look as if you've had *help*.

WILLIAM: I *have* had help, actually. And what I've learnt, in a nutshell, is that it's all about *layering*.

ISABEL: You got so lucky!

WILLIAM: That wasn't *Vanity Fair*'s opinion, as I recall. I think they mentioned something about 'an ability to express the melancholy of the modern condition with tragi-comic insouciance'. *The New Yorker*, incidentally, captioned my portrait 'The man who made the small screen big'.

ISABEL: As a matter of interest… how quickly do you adjust to fame? How long does it take for that first rush of glorious bewilderment… the How Did This Happen to Me? phase… How long does it take before you start to wonder why *even better* things haven't happened to you?

WILLIAM: Seconds.

ISABEL: Do you miss anything about obscurity?

WILLIAM: The legitimacy of complaint.

Beat.

ISABEL: I miss you.

WILLIAM: I know. [*Beat.*] Isabel.

ISABEL: Yes.

WILLIAM: Why did you bring me here?

ISABEL: You know why I brought you here.

WILLIAM: I'm being picked up at seven.

ISABEL: Yes.

WILLIAM: The point is, we need to get on with it.

ISABEL: Ninety. Not much in the scheme of things. A blink.

WILLIAM: I'm here. Aren't I?

ISABEL: You're here because you know I'm—[right]

WILLIAM: *No*. It's a *contract*. You said on the phone—

ISABEL: Yes. All right.

WILLIAM: And by the by, I'm *fourteen* hours behind—

ISABEL: Yes, yes—

WILLIAM: On the phone *at four a.m.* you said—

ISABEL: It's a contract.

WILLIAM: Ninety. And then—

ISABEL: Yes.

WILLIAM: That's it.

ISABEL: Ninety.

WILLIAM: That's it.

ISABEL: That's the contract.

WILLIAM: Just so we're clear. The car is coming for me at seven.

ISABEL: So you said.

WILLIAM: The plane's at ten. Her parents are arriving in Gay Paree as we speak. It's all happening *Dimanche*.

ISABEL: The big day.

WILLIAM: *La grande journée. Exactement.* Charming young Parisian florists are designing floral concepts as we speak. Fancily wrapped presents are assembling themselves on dining tables. Celebrants are performing vocal exercises in preparation. *It's happening.*

ISABEL: Where did you propose?

Beat.

WILLIAM: Here, actually.

ISABEL: Where?

WILLIAM: Do you care?

ISABEL: Yes.

WILLIAM: At Adolpho's.

ISABEL: [*unable to quite disguise her pain*] You proposed at Adolpho's?

WILLIAM: I always go to Adolpho's when I'm in town.

ISABEL: Don't they have an Adolpho's in LA?

WILLIAM: Americans don't understand food. They're quite wonderful in their own way, but when visiting America it's advisable not to eat.

ISABEL: Uh-uh.

WILLIAM: And this city has the best food in the world. Not much happens here, but the citizens do eat well. I lie awake at night thinking about Adolpho's pumpkin and sage ravioli.

ISABEL: So you *do* eat.

WILLIAM: On the sly.

ISABEL: I think about the stuffed zucchini flowers virtually every day. When I was pregnant, I ordered them for entrée *and* main.

WILLIAM: He misses you. He pulls me aside. He likes you better than Vera.

ISABEL: Good old Adolpho.

WILLIAM: For a start, you eat a hell of a lot more than her.

ISABEL: Mildred rang me. Remember her? She's your mother. Sitting in a nursing home with a lot of other women who think they're Princess Diana.

WILLIAM: Thanks for reminding me.

ISABEL: *She* doesn't like Vera at all.

WILLIAM: *She's* not marrying her.

ISABEL: No, alas. How satisfying that would have been on so many levels. Where are you honeymooning?

WILLIAM: St Barths.

ISABEL: So chicly contrary—

WILLIAM: Thank you.

ISABEL: —going somewhere that's over.

WILLIAM: It's not over.

ISABEL: Baby, it's *so* over. Full of decaying, middle-aged men, and young 'actresses' paying for their vacations in blow jobs. [*Beat.*] It's amazing, isn't it? The resilience of hope?

WILLIAM: I want to be happy. *Comprendez?* Too shallow for you? Not enough angst? Not enough poetry? Not enough martyrdom? Some of us just want to be happy. [*Beat.*] Isabel. I'm here because I want, finally, to be done.

ISABEL: Done?

WILLIAM: Over.

ISABEL: It's not over.

WILLIAM: Sometimes *it's just too late*. We can be civilised.

ISABEL: *Love's not civilised.* [*Beat.*] William. You can't escape me.

WILLIAM: I can. I have. Without wishing to hurt you at all, *I just don't love you anymore*.

ISABEL: How easily it trips off the tongue. It's so familiar, somehow. We've all heard it so many times. In life. In books. In movies.

WILLIAM: I just don't love you anymore.

ISABEL: It's almost too familiar, don't you think? When we say the words, do we know what we're saying or are we just looking for something neat? Something to encapsulate… failure.

WILLIAM: Very you. Making something mind-numbingly complex of something dashingly simple. Let me say it again, nice and clear: I Just Don't Love You Anymore.

Beat.

ISABEL: No-one. No-one will love you as I love you.

WILLIAM: Maybe your standards are just lower.

ISABEL: You'd rather be loved less by someone who found you harder to love than me?

WILLIAM: Isn't that the whole wretched thing? Isabel? Isn't that the very reason human beings withstand famine and hijackings and cancer but collapse under the strain of love? We foil happiness because we don't believe we've earned it. [*Beat.*] *I don't love you.*

ISABEL: Why not?

WILLIAM: There's no point.

ISABEL: Tell me.

WILLIAM: *It doesn't matter!*

ISABEL: *Say it!*

WILLIAM: It would be cruel.

ISABEL: [*urgently, she wants to know*] I *want* you to be cruel. If you'd just say what you think, say what you feel, be fucking *brutal,* maybe I'll just go away.

Beat.

WILLIAM: [*gathering force*] All right. Well. You've brought me here, so it has to be said. I loved you. Yes. Once, I loved you. But *I never really liked you.* [*Beat.*] Your judgmentalism. Your high-handed opinions. Your snobbery disguised as intellect. Your voluptuous, somehow unconvincing compassion which always felt more about your *claim* to goodness than genuine feeling. That scent you wore of mildewed Persian rugs and how you never wore a watch. The way you drove, as if the rear-view mirror was just an optional extra. The way you always chose the restaurant but always swapped dishes when mine arrived looking better. The books you read—all those fucking Vikram Seths—as if you were preparing for a dinner party. The people you liked best—the ones who set themselves apart from the ordinary folk. Your *superiority*. I can't stand the way you carry on about how elitist things are when *you're* the fucking elite.

ISABEL: Actually, you like that.

WILLIAM: *No, I don't.* There are lots of things you think I like about you and it's taken me a while myself to realise how ghastly they are. You're such a martyr. All that passive aggressive shit! I was the shallow, vain actor and you were the hallowed wife!

ISABEL: You *are* the shallow, vain actor and I *am* the hallowed wife. I kept us alive, in case you've forgotten.

WILLIAM: For a couple of years. Then there's no end of payback. Every time I looked down at my email, there it was: Stafford and Burkip. Stafford and fucking Burkip, whose business it is to hound husbands into the grave for more and more money.

ISABEL: We didn't have to sell the cottage—that was spite!

WILLIAM: No-one used it.

ISABEL: That was *our* cottage! We *made* her there.

WILLIAM: It was empty all fucking year. You only wanted it because you were notching up acquisitions. You've always been an acquirer. All this arty-farty stuff, all this spiritual crap, your higher consciousness with your Van Eycks and your Bergman festivals. Actually, *you love money*.

ISABEL: [*not arch, she's puzzled*] You're so hard, William. What made you so hard? What is it? That happiness doesn't actually make you that happy?

WILLIAM: Every time I tell you the truth you tell me I'm hard. Actually, *you're* the strategic one. Using words to win. [*Beat.*] Tell me what you want, Isabel. Because it seems to me you love having a reason to complain, like so many women. Instead of getting on with things, you have to find the fucking angst. What is it with women and their infatuation with injustice? It's your *raison d'être*. You want it all ways. You want to rule the world and you want to be looked after. Housewives who want to be CEOs, CEOs who want to be mummies, women who want men to find them hot, women who want men to treat them like men, women who want men to fuck off, women who want cave men with huge dongers, women who wants sooks who *understand* them. Make up your fucking minds. We don't really care *what* you want. *Just choose.*

ISABEL: Funny, isn't it? How the arithmetic of a perfect marriage is when he becomes a bit more of her and she becomes a bit more of him.

WILLIAM: Neither of us was ever good at maths.

ISABEL: Once I said to you, I said: Love is about maintaining certain standards. You laughed. You said I could bring out a t-shirt. Standards of… of delicacy. Is that it? Of refusing to say what might be said because in love one makes a tacit pact to keep certain silences.

Kim Gyngell as William and Melinda Butel as Isabel in the 2008 MTC production. (Photo: Jeff Busby)

WILLIAM: What silences?

ISABEL: Love, honour, fidelity… obedience… they are all secondary. The number one vow is simply the promise not to notice too much. We make that choice in love. We make it easily at first. It's effortless. Because of the fucking and the mystery and the youth. It's easy. And then, one day, it starts. One breaks the pact, the other follows. You say some things, I say some things, and suddenly, we've glimpsed it. The end.

WILLIAM: I like endings. They provoke beginnings.

ISABEL: Tell me, when you walk in to your—to her—the place you're living. When you walk in there and you talk about—what?—one of Vera's favourite topics, say: *Vera*—doesn't the *absence* of things take you over? The worst and the best. The absence of—

WILLIAM: Of—

ISABEL: *The absence of me.*

Beat.

WILLIAM: Well. Sometimes. Perhaps. Only—

ISABEL: Well, then…

WILLIAM: Only…

ISABEL: So…

WILLIAM: I *like* it. The absence of you.

Beat.

ISABEL: And Bea?

WILLIAM: Dead. Gone. Vanished. [*Beat.*] It's okay for things to end, Isabel.

ISABEL: But they don't end. Look at them. [*She looks to the painting.*] You think you see it all in one glance, but at first you see what they want you to see. The way they present themselves to the world. But look long enough and there comes a moment when the truth becomes clear. We have radiography, infra-red, ways of looking so that virtually nothing in a work remains unseen to us. And yet six months after starting I saw it. I'd been working across the panel from left to right, each square inch under microscope-taking weeks. Brush strokes look like mountains. There: an inscription in the paint layer, made when the original paint was wet. 'The only preparation for marriage is marriage.' [*Beat. With quiet tenderness*] We made a world.

WILLIAM: We did.

ISABEL: We had some fun.

WILLIAM: We did.

ISABEL: We loved each other.

WILLIAM: *Yes.*

Beat.

ISABEL: 'You're not teaching us anything.' [*Beat.*] I said. I said, 'You're not teaching us anything'. Wasn't that it?

WILLIAM: No.

ISABEL: And you said, 'Miss Benson, you are deliberately sabotaging this'.

WILLIAM: Isabel. Don't do this.

ISABEL: I hated you. You were so pompous and you were vain and I hate vain men. [*Beat.*] There's something about young men calling young women 'Miss'. It always sounds like a piss-take. And later, I was walking home and I thought to myself, either I'm a pretentious little twat or I'm honest and maybe I'm honest and and you really weren't teaching us anything and if that's the case, you should be in awe of me, in absolute awe of me and therefore in love with me since smart men cannot help falling in love with women they are in awe of. You should be stalking me. You should be walking right behind me, walking behind me, following me not in some sinister way, but rather, because I see you. I see you. I'm clear about you. And being smart, you find that irresistible, that someone sees you clearly. Especially someone with really, really nice tits. [*Beat.*] But you weren't stalking me. I know. Because I looked. So then I went home and I was in my flat and I picked up the phone and I rang. [*Beat. She waits.*] So then I went home and I was in my flat and I picked up the phone and I rang. [*Beat.*] I picked up the phone and I rang.

He relents.

Flashback:

WILLIAM: Hello?

ISABEL: It's me. I think—

Beat.

WILLIAM: [*reluctantly at first*] What?

ISABEL: You should come over.

WILLIAM: What, *now*?

ISABEL: Yes.

WILLIAM: What, *now*?

ISABEL: Yes.

WILLIAM: So you can apologise?

ISABEL: No.

WILLIAM: You disrupted the class. You've done it before. You're irritating.

ISABEL: I know I am, but I think you should come over and take me.

Beat.

WILLIAM: '*Take*' you?

ISABEL: Yes.

WILLIAM: *Where*?

ISABEL: As in 'ravish', you fool. *Tess of the d'Urbervilles.*

WILLIAM: No.

ISABEL: Go on.

WILLIAM: No. No. Are you mad?

ISABEL: Go on.

WILLIAM: I can't come over and… I can't come and… I'm a teacher and you're a student and it's completely inappropriate and besides which, I don't want to. *Tess.*

ISABEL: Why not?

WILLIAM: Because I don't like you.

ISABEL: Okay. All right.

WILLIAM: *At all.*

ISABEL: Okay. But listen, that's no reason not to ravish me. As we all know. Besides which, I don't want—

WILLIAM: What?

ISABEL: I don't—you know—

WILLIAM: No.

ISABEL: *You know!*

WILLIAM: What?

ISABEL: I don't want—

WILLIAM: You don't want—?

ISABEL: Bells and whistles.

WILLIAM: You don't want bells and whistles?

ISABEL: No.

WILLIAM: Well, that's handy, since as it happens I'm all out of bells and whistles—

ISABEL: Just a quick—you know. A roll in the hay. If we had any hay. Which we don't.

WILLIAM: Is this the way you usually find sexual gratification? Make someone very very annoyed and then harass them into servicing your lust?

ISABEL: Listen, Mister Drama Teacher, it's very simple. I'm inviting you over to fuck me.

WILLIAM: Lovely. How nice. Thank you.

ISABEL: You know, any ordinary man would be already ringing the fucking doorbell!

WILLIAM: Call me old-fashioned, but when it comes to performing intimate sexual acts, I prefer not to be brow-beaten.

ISABEL: This is the offer of a lifetime. *You're* the one who should be ringing *me*! *You're* the one who should be trying to seduce *me*. I'm the one who should be listening to you leave plaintive messages on my machine. I'm the one who should be ringing my girlfriends complaining about your unwanted advances. I'm the one who should start out totally despising you and then slowly, slowly be won over by you when you start singing bad pop songs outside my window or organising planes to sky-write 'Marry Me'. I'm the one who should come around to letting you *have your way* with me. That's the way it's always been done. The girl *is persuaded.* The boy *persuades*. [*Beat.*] Why won't you come?

WILLIAM: I told you, I don't like you.

ISABEL: What is it you don't like about me?

WILLIAM: You're annoying. You're a show-off. And you drive a Torana.

ISABEL: And?

WILLIAM: I'm scared.

ISABEL: What are you scared of?

WILLIAM: Everything.

ISABEL: That's not an answer.

WILLIAM: I'm scared of finding that your place is full of self-help books and old yoghurt. I'm scared that when I see you up close, your tits aren't that big after all. I'm scared that you seem interesting at a distance, but up close you're just weird, or even disturbed. I'm scared that all over your flat you've got blown-up photos of me going about my life unsuspecting and that you hate men because you're uncle molested you and I'm the one you've chosen to wreak revenge on. I'm scared you have AIDS. I'm scared you want a baby and you get pregnant and then I've suddenly got something with my DNA moving into the spare room *that's never, ever going to move out*. I'm scared your old boyfriend is a large, deranged crack-head. I'm scared that you're really appalling in bed and that you whistle 'I Am Woman' while your come. I'm scared that you're unbelievably hot in bed and I'm intimidated and realise that I'm shit ordinary. I'm scared you pray, or knit, or—or, make really horrible art out of old candles. I'm scared you're deluded about yourself and I can see it and I pity you. I'm scared you talk too much about Europe or New British Writing. I'm scared I might love you and then I'm totally fucked.

Beat.

ISABEL: What if I promise not to whistle? [*Beat. Saucily*] And then you came over.

WILLIAM: Yes I did.

ISABEL: You came over and you—

WILLIAM: Yes.

ISABEL: I showed you my etchings.

WILLIAM: You did.

ISABEL: You couldn't resist me, after all.

WILLIAM: 'Resist'? Mmm. 'Avoid', perhaps. You positioned yourself in the middle of my flight path. If I didn't bed you I was going to have to run you over.

ISABEL: *You couldn't resist me!*

WILLIAM: It was the absence of bad candle-art that clinched it. My aphrodisiac was gratitude.

ISABEL: When you first introduced me to Arthur, you were *proud.*

WILLIAM: I knew Arthur would like you. Yes, I *was* proud.

ISABEL: I was a 'class act'.

WILLIAM: My last girlfriend kept a packet of cigarettes under her t-shirt sleeve, so let's face it, anything was going to be an improvement.

ISABEL: You liked that I was from a 'good' family.

WILLIAM: You think I liked feeling you up because your mother wore pearls and cooked French sauces?

ISABEL: Yes. Yes. Her French sauces made me saucy. In a French way. You liked it because you thought that you were somehow smudging me. Grubbying me up. And that gave you a bit of a charge.

WILLIAM: Did it?

ISABEL: The affected open-mindedness of the educated upper middle class. It *rocked* you. It made you feel sophisticated.

WILLIAM: [*correcting her*] What I really liked, if you must know, was the way you swore. Ex private school girls have this way of swearing which is incredibly erotic. Those peachy, post-braces lip-glossed mouths used to curling themselves around school hymns, uttering naughty words.

ISABEL: The other thing you liked was that I didn't use sex as flattery. I didn't pretend you were pleasing me when you weren't, so when I *was* excited, I really *was* excited. You liked that.

WILLIAM: Not really. What women don't understand. What you lot don't really *get* is that we *like* it when you pretend. We *prefer* it when you pretend. It's so much more time efficient, for a start, than spending hours twiddling your knobs and getting nowhere. Just do your Oscar-winning number, thank you very much.

ISABEL: You definitely liked my stories.

WILLIAM: Fair enough. When it comes to pornographic anecdotes, you were the one.

ISABEL: You liked the way they revved me up. That made you excited…

WILLIAM: I did like the one about the suburbanites who invite the neighbours over for fondue. I tell you what, if the industry utilised your creative skills, there'd be a revolution in cheese consumption.

ISABEL: You also liked the one about the cinema.

WILLIAM: You can't go wrong with a cinema. You can't go wrong with a French maid. They're a dead cert.

ISABEL: Yes, but I had the detail. It can't be easy being a French maid when you're a German dog-walker.

WILLIAM: Vera's not a dog-walker.

ISABEL: Okay, sorry. The German *actress* with a Dalmatian, a Pomeranian, two Jack Russells and a Poodle.

WILLIAM: It's temporary. She *is* an actress.

ISABEL: So you don't want me to think she *walks dogs* but you don't mind me thinking she's German.

WILLIAM: She *is* German.

ISABEL: She wear a uniform, then? You always liked a woman in uniform.

WILLIAM: Only that one time.

ISABEL: I went to a great deal of effort. It wasn't just a matter of the outfit. I method acted. I *was* an Italian traffic cop.

WILLIAM: I know you were.

ISABEL: *Se parcheggi davanti alla fontana di Trevi devi lascarti schiaffeggare al meno un po'. Non sono io a fare le regole.*

WILLIAM: [*memorised*] 'If you park in front of the Trevi fountain, you're going to have to allow me to slap you around a little. I don't make the rules.' I admit, you were good.

ISABEL: It was destiny.

WILLIAM: 'It'?

ISABEL: We. Us. We were. It happened. Marjorie met Michael at a bus stop, had me, I went to *that* university, Theatre Studies. I *hate* Theatre Studies. I was only ever interested in art, but I had to choose an extra subject and suddenly there you were, pretending to be some kind of expert. Because you were a crap soccer player and a crap guitar player, you failed every audition and you had nothing left to be except a drama teacher. We came together. *Destiny*. We're preordained, baby.

WILLIAM: What about Vera? She was my destiny, *next*. Why shouldn't I respect that?

ISABEL: You two aren't destined.

WILLIAM: Oh. Oh. I see. You and I. *We* are. But she and I…

ISABEL: She's *chosen*. To render me invisible. She's not written into your story, from the start. She's a walking, talking conscious choice.

WILLIAM: Well, even if she is a choice, she's a good choice.

ISABEL: She's not good.

WILLIAM: Believe me, she's good.

ISABEL: Does she make you hard?

WILLIAM: As Rock.

ISABEL: How's her storytelling?

WILLIAM: Not as good as yours.

ISABEL: So.

WILLIAM: But she makes a really gorgeous noise when she comes. Sort of like a Norwegian air hostess eating a lychee.

ISABEL: [*indignant*] I can do that! You just never asked!

WILLIAM: *Vera didn't need to be asked.*

ISABEL: Do they watch?

WILLIAM: Who?

ISABEL: The two Jack Russells, the Pomeranian and the Poodle?

WILLIAM: No, but the Dalmatian fetches us the ciggies when it's all over.

ISABEL: If you're going to take up with an actress, why couldn't it be Catherine Zeta-Jones?

WILLIAM: Believe me, she has a face like a used tea bag first thing in the morning.

ISABEL: You've seen Catherine Zeta-Jones first thing in the morning!

WILLIAM: No comment.

ISABEL: How do you know?

WILLIAM: *I know.*

ISABEL: [*absorbing*] Is it true?

WILLIAM: No. But I've found that nothing makes a woman happier than hearing Catherine Zeta-Jones looks like a prawn cracker.

They smile.

Light change.

Flashback:

ISABEL: Hello. [*She waits.*] 'Hello', said you. Here you are.

WILLIAM: [*reluctantly*] I'm not sure why.

ISABEL: Disingenuous.

WILLIAM: Five syllables. That's four more than any word that's come out of your mouth all term.

ISABEL: I've been saving them up.

WILLIAM: For when?

ISABEL: For when you're standing on my doorstep. Looking—*lugubrious*.

WILLIAM: Nice.

ISABEL: Come in. Just be careful of my candle-wax sculptures of vaginas.

WILLIAM: Oh, shit.

ISABEL: *I'm joking!*

WILLIAM: Has anyone told you, you have an unusual way of signalling your availability?

ISABEL: For what?

WILLIAM: Well.

ISABEL: You've come to help me with my Pinter project, haven't you?

WILLIAM: [*laughing*] Your 'Pinter' project?

ISABEL: In class? You said you'd be happy to—Am I wrong?

WILLIAM: [*confused*] Your 'Pinter' project?

ISABEL: Harold Pinter British playwright 1937 dash 2008.

WILLIAM: [*dawning on him, horribly*] Your Pinter project?

ISABEL: Yes, I mean, that's why you're here, isn't it?

WILLIAM: Well—

ISABEL: Why else would you be here?

WILLIAM: [*confused*] Well—didn't we just have a phone conversation?

ISABEL: A phone conversation?

WILLIAM: Yes.

ISABEL: With me?

WILLIAM: You [*now doubting*] invited me over?

ISABEL: What?

WILLIAM: Just—?

ISABEL: When—?

WILLIAM: I'm sorry. I thought—

ISABEL: What? Not—?

WILLIAM: No!

ISABEL: *Oh, my God!* You didn't think—?

WILLIAM: Of course not!

ISABEL: You're my teacher! You could be sacked!

Beat as she lets him suffer. Then slowly she lifts her sweater up and off, revealing her bare breasts.

WILLIAM: You're horrible.

As he puts his hands on her breasts:

ISABEL: I know. But up close, they *are* big, aren't they?

Brief blackout.

Out of the darkness: the sound of ISABEL *whistling 'I Am Woman'.*

Lights up.

Beat. Post coital.

WILLIAM: *That* is what I would call worthwhile.

ISABEL: Worthwhile?

WILLIAM: It's good to see finally that there's something you're good at.

ISABEL: Is that so?

WILLIAM: Well, you're an awful student, let's face it.

ISABEL: Irredeemable?

WILLIAM: I'm afraid so. But *this*. This you can do!

ISABEL: Well, thank you for the accolades.

WILLIAM: A definite A-minus.

Beat.

ISABEL: You're *grading* me?

WILLIAM: Habit.

Beat.

ISABEL: [*unable to help herself*] What's the minus for?

WILLIAM: Impertinence. All those directions: 'Faster, slower, right hand down, in a bit, in a bit'. I felt like I was trying to do a reverse park.

ISABEL: I'll try to improve.

They smile.

Anyway, I don't want to act. Why would I want to 'act'? I want to live! I'm dropping Drama at the end of the semester and doing the Conservation course.

WILLIAM: Good. Good choice. We'll miss you.

ISABEL: You'll be seeing quite a bit of me at the ethics tribunal. The one you'll be grilled at over bedding your comely students.

WILLIAM: Not plural.

ISABEL: That's *your* story. I do think your self-discovery workshops are complete rubbish, by the way.

WILLIAM: Oh, thanks!

ISABEL: And don't think you're a life changer.

WILLIAM: Life changer?

ISABEL: One of those teachers. You're not gifted.

WILLIAM: No. But as a drama teacher, I'm an excellent actor.

ISABEL: You're acting?

WILLIAM: Come on! The glasses. The well-timed explosions about 'mediocrity'. The jacket with the elbow patches.

ISABEL: I hate you.

WILLIAM: Hate's an ugly word.

ISABEL: Not as ugly as 'muesli'.

WILLIAM: True.

ISABEL: 'Muesli' is the ugliest word in the English language.

WILLIAM: Yet people still eat it. Interesting.

ISABEL: Don't you hate anyone?

WILLIAM: Only Deborah Kerr.

ISABEL: You hate Deborah Kerr?

WILLIAM: Have you ever really *looked* at her? *Satan.*

Beat.

ISABEL: Who is Deborah Kerr?

They smile.

WILLIAM: I'm too old for you.

ISABEL: You're not old.

WILLIAM: I'm appallingly, poignantly old. You only love me because I'm rich and powerful.

ISABEL: Funny.

WILLIAM: I'm so old I remember someone explaining this new thing called 'email'. Imagine that. One day my great grandchildren will reflect on that in stunned silence. It'll be like saying I had tea with the last Tsar before the revolution.

ISABEL: Fuck me again.

WILLIAM: Not *again.*

ISABEL: Again and again and again.

Light change.

Beat.

WILLIAM: Forty-nine.

ISABEL: You know, don't you, that sexually speaking, a woman only really wants that first tiny moment of being wanted? The sex itself is really… well, let's face it. Sex is utterly and completely overrated except for maybe three times in your life.

WILLIAM: What?

ISABEL: You don't agree?

WILLIAM: Come on! We were married! *You* were married to *me*.

ISABEL: Yes.

WILLIAM: And you didn't enjoy sex?

ISABEL: Yes. Yes. Of course I did. But you know, the act itself was secondary to *being desired*. A woman's sexual excitement is totally and completely controlled by *how she is received*.

WILLIAM: My God! Come back, Germaine, all is forgiven!

ISABEL: The look that passes from a lustful man to the object of his interest—that look *is* the female orgasm.

WILLIAM: So the other orgasm—what? Doesn't exist?

ISABEL: Oh, sure. It exists. But it's the punctuation, not the poetry.

WILLIAM: Not all women feel that way.

ISABEL: No. No. I'm sorry. *All* women feel that way.

WILLIAM: Vera doesn't feel that way.

ISABEL: [*smugly*] Ask her.

Anxious beat as he contemplates it.

WILLIAM: [*hurt, shocked*] You didn't enjoy sex with me?

ISABEL: At the start. But later, to be honest, you were just a little too genteel.

WILLIAM: What?

ISABEL: If a man reveals no hidden aspect of his character when making love, a woman always wonders what's there.

WILLIAM: I was *too nice*?

ISABEL: Women don't like their lovers too well-mannered. Otherwise, you might as well play cards.

WILLIAM: *Sex with me was like playing cards?*

ISABEL: I kept wondering: Who is he really? As if your most unruly self was just a little bit afraid. Didn't you feel that yourself?

WILLIAM: [*shocked*] I—No. No. [*Beat.*] Why didn't you tell me?

ISABEL: I couldn't *shape* you into the lover I wanted. Analysis kills desire. And does it matter? Really? I'm sure there were times we closed our eyes and I was your young Catherine Deneuve and you were my Jean-Claude Van Damme.

WILLIAM: [*horrified*] *You thought of Jean-Claude Van Damme?*

ISABEL: He was playing an art conservator in a new film and I was his adviser.

WILLIAM: And who was the casting agent? Mickey fucking Mouse? No-one would cast Jean-Claude Van Damme as an art conservator!

ISABEL: *I would.* And he adored me because none of his other girlfriends ate.

WILLIAM: *You're wrong.* I know how well we… I remember how deeply we… Not always, but at our best—*yes.* We were great…

ISABEL: [*quietly*] Were we?

WILLIAM: I… I loved sex with you.

ISABEL: Maybe your standards are just lower.

WILLIAM: Remember when we hiked—Cradle Mountain—when the storm hit and we—

ISABEL: Yes.

WILLIAM: That time after the thing in the place when they left—

ISABEL: Yes.

WILLIAM: And the French B and B, in the attic, with the dust mites and we—

ISABEL: Yes.

WILLIAM: Well?

ISABEL: What?

WILLIAM: [*tenderly, caught in the memory*] Well, that was wonderful. That was—wasn't that wonderful?

ISABEL: [*with very quiet triumph*] Yes.

Beat.

WILLIAM: Isabel.

ISABEL: William—

WILLIAM: I know what you're doing—

ISABEL: Do you?

WILLIAM: You think I'll—

ISABEL: Just—

WILLIAM: No. *Please.* It's over. I have a life, Isabel. That's not about you.

ISABEL: I guess, acting is a useful pursuit if you are sick of being yourself.

WILLIAM: Do you know what? I don't even remember who I am. And that gives me enormous pleasure. I am the actor. I'm 'that guy in that series'. I'm Mister Golden Artichoke and I'm *happy for me.*

ISABEL: And you're brilliant at it! I mean it. You *do* make the small screen big. At the same time as making real life small. You're a genius illusionist.

WILLIAM: I fell out of love.

ISABEL: And Vera? You love Vera of course.

WILLIAM: She's beautiful.

ISABEL: She's the kind of beautiful men think is beautiful and women know isn't really beautiful.

WILLIAM: Objectively, without any opinion involved at all, she's chronologically—*young.*

ISABEL: And you like young?

WILLIAM: *I love it.* What's *not* to like? Young's *always* good. *We all like it.*

ISABEL: And you love her?

WILLIAM: I'm marrying her on Sunday!

ISABEL: You love Vera?

WILLIAM: Her family's arriving in Paris. Laden with toasters.

ISABEL: You love her, then?

WILLIAM: Of course I love her!

ISABEL: [*sharing rather than arguing*] That's why you're standing here now. Here. In front of me. Three days before the wedding. Giving me my ninety. Because you're so in love. [*Beat.*] I pity her. Because one day, the real William is going to emerge. Mister Loquacious Talk Show Guest is going to turn into something real. There he is—the man who suavely joked his way through courtship, someone who *famously*, never allowed anything to really *get* to him—suddenly overwhelmed by the full savage burden of inexplicable *life.* He's tried to shake it off, but it will not let him go. The wife he left. The daughter he lost. All they felt for him and he for them, the dogged archive of a family. He's tried. He's run, *fast.* But whenever he tries to sleep, there it is, the memory of who he once was and who belonged to him. And one day, Vera is going to come back to the *Georges Cinq*, laden with shopping bags, and there he will be: *A man who has spent his entire life denying the force of his emotions and suddenly: they've taken their revenge.*

WILLIAM: Do emotions take revenge?

ISABEL: It's *all* they do.

WILLIAM: [*angry*] You're so certain, aren't you, Isabel?

ISABEL: You think you can pretend with me? *With me?* You went to hell once and you went there with me. *I remind you of hell*. And she comes along. She's pretty, she's impressed by you *and she's never been to hell*. Love? Love, is it?

WILLIAM: [*furious*] *Yes*. And, I tell you what. Something else I love about Vera. [*Beat.*] She's never had a child. [*Beat.*] *I love that*. Women who've had children: they become more interesting at the same time as less compelling. *They've glimpsed their own redundancy*. They give birth and something in them dies: *the sexuality of their own importance. Men love that*. Just so you know.

Beat as she takes in the brutality of this.

ISABEL: And what about *you*? For *her*? How long are *you* going to be dazzling to *her*?

WILLIAM: You think I'm going to analyse passion? With you?

ISABEL: You're right. *Passion doesn't last long enough to explain.*

Beat. WILLIAM *moves towards the door.*

WILLIAM: I'd love to stay and all that. Discuss art. Replay old records. Tear each other to shreds. But I should get going. Getting married, as I am. In another hemisphere. And all that.

ISABEL: No!

WILLIAM: I'm off. Have a wonderful life. Send me a postcard in about fifteen years. From St Barths. I'm sure it will be back in by then.

ISABEL: The car's not coming for another forty minutes.

WILLIAM: I think you'll find. If you look. That the car is there.

ISABEL: [*alarmed*] He's waiting?

WILLIAM: He's reading Proust. So I'm sure he'll be ready for an interruption.

ISABEL: [*distraught, but trying to stay calm*] William, you promised me.

WILLIAM: It's a funny old world, isn't it? When your driver reads Proust?

ISABEL: [*with growing desperation*] *You promised me. You said—you promised me. You promised me, William. You promised me. William. William. William. Ninety. You said. You said. You gave me ninety.*

Beat.

WILLIAM: [*relenting*] Forty-one left, then I get my plane. Because I'm getting married. On Sunday.

Beat. He sits down again.

ISABEL: You didn't propose to me at Adolpho's.

WILLIAM: No.

ISABEL: *Unfortunately*. You took advantage—

WILLIAM: Well, that's what I do. Let's be realistic.

ISABEL: I was a captive audience.

The sound of recorded applause.

Flashback:

WILLIAM *bows towards* ISABEL.

WILLIAM: Ladies and gentlemen. Thank you… Thank you… Thanks for attending tonight's performance. Before you go, however, I wanted to ask the young lady in the floral dress and nice breasts sitting in D16 if she'd marry me.

Beat.

ISABEL: What?

WILLIAM: Isabel Louise Benson. [*Peering into the lights*] *Are you there?*

ISABEL: *No!*

WILLIAM: Will you marry me?

ISABEL: [*putting on a funny voice*] She's not here. She's gone home!

WILLIAM: Will you? Isabel? Will you marry me? [*Beat. Pompously*] Will you be my wife?

ISABEL: [*to herself*] Jesus Christ! [*Yelling*] *No!*

WILLIAM: What?

ISABEL: No!

WILLIAM: You won't marry me?

ISABEL: Not *now*.

WILLIAM: I thought you'd like it. I thought it would be a cute anecdote you could tell the grandchildren.

ISABEL: I don't want a cute anecdote. I want someone wild and brilliant and terrifying.

WILLIAM: *But that's me!* I'm actually *deeply terrifying*. I'm dark and menacing. I'm a melancholic genius. *I hate cute anecdotes!* I'm a brooding alcoholic weirdo. I read… Dostoyevsky. In Russian. Every night. I rage about the vacuousness of the modern condition. I keep a knife under my pillow and I never laugh. Come on… come on… *marry me.* I'll put my DNA on good behaviour. [*Beat.*] Will you?

Beat.

ISABEL: [*softening*] Maybe.

Beat.

WILLIAM: *Maybe?* [*Beat.*] What about the fat lady in the beanie in F24? Doing anything for the rest of your life?

ISABEL: [*terse*] Oh, *all right!*

Applause.

Light change.

Beat. They smile.

We're late.

Light change.

Flashback:

WILLIAM: I really think I need more training. It's a delicate operation in a notoriously dangerous combat zone with major security issues and an enemy who takes no prisoners. I'm going in alone and under-prepared.

ISABEL: My parents are actually quite nice.

WILLIAM: Your father reminds me of Himmler.

ISABEL: Nice.

WILLIAM: It's the eyes.

ISABEL: Try not to use that as your opening gambit.

WILLIAM: [*delaying*] Isabel, Isabel, Isabel. 'It must have been cold there in my shadow.'

ISABEL: Where?

WILLIAM: 'To never have sunlight on your face.'

ISABEL: What?

WILLIAM: 'You were content to let me shine, that's your way.'

ISABEL: What on earth are you talking about? Are you drunk?

WILLIAM: 'You always walked a step behind.'

ISABEL: Behind *who*?

WILLIAM: [*breaking into singing*] 'Did you ever know that you're my hero, and everything I would like to be? I can fly higher than an eagle, for you are the wind beneath my wings.'

ISABEL: [*smiling*] Well, that's all very well, but I don't really *want* to be your *wind*.

WILLIAM: [*heartfelt*] I love you.

ISABEL: [*dismissive, but touched*] Oh yes, yes, yes…

WILLIAM: I just know your father is going to ask me a trick question. 'Who was the more popular male writer: George Eliot or Henry Handel Richardson?' Something to prove my complete and utter inadequacy. And then he'll ask me to sniff the wine and I'm going to have to come up with something like 'fruity bouquet' or 'tinges of blackberry'.

ISABEL: You know what, let's not go—

WILLIAM: Don't be ridiculous.

ISABEL: I've changed my mind. I don't want to marry you.

WILLIAM: Oh, that's what they all say.

She laughs.

ISABEL: I want you to know the only reason I agreed was out of pity.

WILLIAM: I know, but, sadly, it's the best offer I'm likely to get. Also I have a thing for art history types, as you know. It's so grown-up. It's so velvet-robed, pale-skinned, intellectual. It's so fancypants. [*Beat.*] They'll hate me.

ISABEL: They'll love you—

WILLIAM: No, they won't.

ISABEL: No, they won't. But they'll respect my right to marry you.

WILLIAM: No, they won't—

ISABEL: Well, no they won't, but I'll marry you anyway.

WILLIAM: *Rebel*.

ISABEL: *Inciter*.

Light change.

The weight of the memory affects her.

[*Quietly and building*] It's not enough, is it? One life is not—

WILLIAM: What?

ISABEL: Not—

WILLIAM: *What?*

ISABEL: *Enough.*

WILLIAM: One life is not enough?

ISABEL: You gather experience blind. You think: At some point, I'll understand how things are done: loving, learning, parenting, fucking. At some point surely I'll know how to do them well. Then one day as you're walking into the newsagency on a spring afternoon, you realise that *now you know*. Somehow life has gathered about you and it's *registered*. You're not a newcomer anymore. You look at young people and they suddenly seem *young*. They annoy you. They don't understand how much they don't know with their piercings and their knee-jerk anti-authoritarianism. You want to say: Grow up! Start reading the Property Sections, start procreating, show some tenderness towards your parents. Grow Up! Like me. And then suddenly, you feel the low-down deep ache of loss. You've gained wisdom, but other things are vanishing from you. *Your own raw capacity for discovery*. Things don't startle you, anymore. The swift sense of outrage at injustice or unkindness—it's over. You've become a shrugger. You've been around the block. You've survived the worst that is survivable and now, nothing really excites you. There's nothing evangelical about your talents. No lust to make your imprint on the world. You're a known quantity. And faintly, faintly, through the hum of your own inner whitegoods, your functioning internal appliances: humour, confidence, intelligence, through the hum of those reliable furnishings is a small penetrating alarm that you cannot silence. *It will not be silenced.* And then, before you even realise, it has captivated you. The longing to be new again! To *un*learn! To jettison all the wisdom, the catalogue of recriminations, mischance, regret, failed choices, uncontrolled outcomes—all of it. Get rid of it! And find, in some sweet-faced other, the opportunity to *begin again*. [*Beat.*] She is entirely *of the moment*.

WILLIAM: All right. She *is*. She *is* the moment.

ISABEL: And us?

WILLIAM: We were the glorious moment and then our moment vanished.

ISABEL: And history?

WILLIAM: I don't want history. *I want to be brutally alive.*

They lock eyes. Long beat.

And what about you, Isabel? Any moments—? In all this time—?

ISABEL: No.

WILLIAM: No? Surely—?

ISABEL: There was—

WILLIAM: [*surprised, not in a good way*] Oh?

ISABEL: A brief—

WILLIAM: There *was*? That's *great*.

ISABEL: A brief—

WILLIAM: Oh yes, *encounter*. Why don't you ever hear marriage described as a *long* encounter? Do encounters have to be brief?

ISABEL: There was some—

WILLIAM: Was there?

ISABEL: Interest. But *I* wasn't interested. In the end.

WILLIAM: In him?

ISABEL: In being interesting.

WILLIAM: Shame. Who was he?

ISABEL: He loved me.

WILLIAM: Did he?

ISABEL: I believe he did. You could tell in the way that he—

WILLIAM: What?

ISABEL: Touched—

WILLIAM: Really? Well, it sounds good. You're too fussy, that's your problem. Who was he?

ISABEL: No-one you… [*beat*] *like*. It felt good to be loved. In your wake.

WILLIAM: Happy for you. You *needed* that.

ISABEL: It seems so unfair. These men—it's as if they trail men like you. The lovers and the leavers. They realise that's their place, to come in where you vacate.

WILLIAM: Works for everyone.

ISABEL: Except, disgustingly, most women would rather be left dazzlingly than worshipped tenderly.

WILLIAM: What did he do?

ISABEL: He was in journalism.

WILLIAM: Like Arthur. A handsome hack. What area?

Beat.

ISABEL: Sports.
WILLIAM: Huh! Like Arthur. [*Beat.*] What was his name?
ISABEL: Arthur.

Long beat.

WILLIAM: *You had an affair with my brother?*
ISABEL: Well, I always wanted to.
WILLIAM: What?
ISABEL: But somehow, it didn't seem right… while I was married to you.
WILLIAM: Isn't that funny? [*Beat.*] Are you sure it was Arthur?
ISABEL: He's incredibly sexy. It's something to do with the freckles and the sports thing. Men who are into sports… it's just so *boyish.* It's such a *happy* pursuit. Because it's so meaningless and temporary. One week their club is number one, the next week they're losers, and on it goes. A bowl of pasta and a match and the odd intimate act. Those men… they have it all over the nicely turned-out intellectuals who take a girl out to dinner and talk about how Martin Amis has 'gone off'. You always thought you were so superior to Arthur because you were arty, never realising that women *flipped* for him.
WILLIAM: *Women flipped for Arthur?*
ISABEL: I used to have this sexual fantasy that you *leant* me to him.
WILLIAM: *What?*
ISABEL: He dropped in at the house late one night and you noticed the way he looked at me and you said: Go ahead. *Take my wife.*
WILLIAM: Take my wife?
ISABEL: And he took me upstairs to our bedroom while you sat downstairs watching *Vanya on 42nd Street. Making notes.*

Beat.

WILLIAM: How? How then?
ISABEL: A year ago, I bumped into Arthur at the theatre. *Waiting for Godot* done by Canadians. The kind of thing you once got excited about, before you went all *Who Weekly.*
WILLIAM: That's so typical! So *you.* Famous for your loyalty. Pious. Pale. Lovely. Faithful to the last. But once you choose infidelity, it's with my *sibling*! Jesus, Isabel, I wouldn't have slept with your sister!
ISABEL: Only because I don't have a sister.
WILLIAM: *If you did.* Why *brief* encounter?

ISABEL: Oh. Well. He's modest, Arthur. And you know I never really go for modest.

WILLIAM: Is that so?

ISABEL: No. I like a certain amount of self-delusion in a man. It's so entertaining.

WILLIAM: And you didn't have that with Arthur?

ISABEL: He's rigorously self-aware. Far too smart. And he could make observations on ordinary things that would make me cry.

WILLIAM: He'd make you cry?

ISABEL: Yes—you know—about the drycleaner's face or a teenage girl standing at a railway crossing [*Beat.*] And of course, he knew Bea.

WILLIAM: Yes.

ISABEL: William, you weren't there.

WILLIAM: No.

ISABEL: And he was.

WILLIAM: Yes.

ISABEL: You both sweep your hair off your face the same way. You both like pecan pie and hate snow peas. He was the you you have when you don't have you.

WILLIAM: All this time I thought it was specifically me you liked. I didn't realise it was just a general attraction to the family gene pool.

ISABEL: Unnerved you, have I?

WILLIAM: Not at all. It's just I'm—I thought this was all about how you couldn't get over me. The great love. And all that.

ISABEL: [*angry*] Is that it, William? There's always one in a couple, isn't there? Who cares more about what they trigger than what they feel.

WILLIAM: [*incensed*] Isabel. Whatever happened afterwards, I *loved*! I lay beside you, *passionately*, *faithfully*. I loved you *frantically*.

ISABEL: *Well, if you loved me so much, why the fuck did you go?*

Beat. Intense. Silent.

It wasn't Arthur I wanted, was it? *It was the best version of you.* [*Beat.*] The William who had lightness and joy. Who stood on the roof of parliament and sang to me. Who bought me twenty-nine blow-up pelicans and put them on my lawn on my birthday. Who had some fantastic irreverent soundtrack to world events that lit up conversation like a flare. [*Beat.*] You were an original. There was no-one quite like you. When I kissed you, you tasted of Camel cigarettes and mint and I thought: *There's only one and he's mine.*

Beat, he's affected deeply.

February twenty-fifth at six p.m.

WILLIAM: Do you have to?

ISABEL: Ivory silk and sandals.

WILLIAM: Isabel.

ISABEL: I was very simple and unaffected before everyone got simple and unaffected.

WILLIAM: Let's leave it alone.

ISABEL: Your shirt matched… We matched. Your speech to me was…

WILLIAM: [*laughing*] … All the important things that happened on February twenty-fifth.

ISABEL: The day the world record was set for a snowmobile, the day the Nicaraguans voted out the Sandinistas, the day Buddy Holly recorded 'That'll Be the Day', the day Hitler got German citizenship, the day the 'insanity plea' was first used to prove innocence, the day Cassius Clay defeated Sonny Liston, the day Pammy Anderson had Tommy Lee arrested and the day *we got married.*

WILLIAM: You got drunk. You were *very* drunk when we got on the flight.

ISABEL: You *need* to be for Alitalia. They advise you. When you book.

WILLIAM: We arrived in Rome at five a.m. We nearly froze to death waiting for a hotel room.

ISABEL: We took the cab straight from Fiumicino to the Pantheon. We stood in front of it.

WILLIAM: It must have been minus something.

ISABEL: We held each other. I had a ring. We were married. It was the Pantheon. We cried.

Beat as they remember.

Light change.

Flashback:

It's the Pantheon.

WILLIAM: The biggest dome in the world.

ISABEL: It's the Pantheon. We're standing in front of it.

WILLIAM: It's the Pantheon.

ISABEL: Here we are.

WILLIAM: The Pantheon!

A moment of huge tenderness:

ISABEL: *Husband.*

WILLIAM: *Wife.*

ISABEL: [*breaking the moment*] It's fucking freezing and we're married.

WILLIAM: We're married.

ISABEL: We're *married*!

WILLIAM: How the fuck did *that* happen?

ISABEL: You stood on a stage and humiliated me in public.

WILLIAM: You should have another coat on. You're going to catch a cold.

ISABEL: Who cares? *We're married.* Colds aren't a problem anymore. *Nothing's* a problem. If you asked me to I'd take off all my clothes right now. I'd dance a jig. I'd eat squid ink pasta without cutlery. I'd do *anything* for you.

WILLIAM: You were so drunk on the plane, I made a resolution about when we got home.

ISABEL: What was that?

WILLIAM: I'd divorce you. [*Beat.*] *Dipsomaniac.*

ISABEL: Buy me a cappuccino? My stomach's *ice.*

WILLIAM: Well, we're here for twelve days and unfortunately we can only afford three coffees. If you want the first now, I suppose you can. But don't come crawling back to me after the third.

ISABEL: *Sadist.*

WILLIAM: *Glutton.*

Light change.

ISABEL: It was when they first computerised credit cards. We were over the limit. The only places we could eat were the ones that still had the manual machines.

WILLIAM: Poverty and Caravaggios.

ISABEL: We seemed to be in a perpetual state of excitement. What were we excited about? In those days?

WILLIAM: Our potential.

ISABEL: Ah yes. 'Young people's wealth'.

WILLIAM: Frankly, I think it's overrated. There are certain things it's really a pleasure to leave behind. Lentils. Boz Scaggs. Potential. Far better to jettison it. Unnecessary ballast. Let it wash up on the shores of someone else's youth.

ISABEL: So that's what we were excited about. Potential.

WILLIAM: And pizza.

ISABEL: Oh yes, not forgetting pizza.

WILLIAM: And sex.

ISABEL: That place that opened onto the street near the Piazza Navona. Potato and rosemary, hot in our hands. We didn't have any money. I don't know how we did it.

WILLIAM: You bludgeoned me. As usual.

ISABEL: I said to you: I Have To Go to Rome for My Honeymoon, and somehow we did.

WILLIAM: Goethe said: The only preparation for Rome is Rome.

Beat.

ISABEL: That was before we were tattooed by life. It was all ahead. We talked about having a child. You said: Let's hope it has my looks and your brains.

WILLIAM: Or failing that, your looks and brains and my knees. Because my knees are really extraordinarily good. I used to be a knee model. You can laugh. But I was in hot demand by sock makers.

Light change.

Flashback:

Hello you.

ISABEL: Hello you.

WILLIAM: That was sneaky. Going into labour while I was out of town.

ISABEL: Frankly, the idea of you in the labour suite was frightening. I think the contractions were entirely opportunistic.

WILLIAM: It was—?

ISABEL: Oh, lovely. I tried very hard to commune with the primal journey, the spiritual significance of new life etcetera etcetera but all I could really think about was how much I wanted to kill you. You'd think, to even things up a bit, that a female *orgasm* would last twenty-seven hours.

WILLIAM: [*with huge tenderness*] *Genius.*

They smile. He looks at the baby.

She's beautiful. She's like a tiny… squashed… wrinkled… hairless… purple version of you.

ISABEL: Beatrice Alice, meet your father.

Long silence. They are overcome.

WILLIAM: As I was in the cab from the airport, angels started singing.

ISABEL: Really?

WILLIAM: Absolutely. They had teeny-tiny trumpets. Lightning flashed and then the skies turned blue. Gold dust floated down over the city, did you see it?

ISABEL: Perhaps I did.

WILLIAM: Tides stopped. Dogs in suburban kennels started howling. Soap operas on telly were interrupted by newsflashes. Trains came to a halt in their tunnels. School children looked amazed out of their classroom windows at the trumpeting angels, atheists paused irritably at the provocation, coffee machines gurgled to a stop, traffic lights flashed amber, morning radio hosts stopped their stupid commentaries, ordinary civilians ran out onto the streets and fell to their knees. Something in the Amazon happened with butterflies and dead crops in Ecuador sprang green roots. And [*looking at* ISABEL] *it's all* [*beat*] *your* [*beat*] *fault.*

Light change.

WILLIAM *is affected by the memory.*

I'd forgotten I remembered that.

Beat.

ISABEL: It's a tricky little thing, sex. Isn't it? Do it properly and you never have time to do it again.

WILLIAM: You were brave.

ISABEL: I was so brave. It seemed so weird to me, that I had invented something that was partly you. [*Touched*] What a trick that is.

They smile.

WILLIAM: Everything went swimmingly until you went to Aarhus for the conference. From that point on, I was sinking.

ISABEL: It was only for a week!

WILLIAM: If it had actually been documented, I'd have been on the cover of the Sunday supplements. I'd be on the inspirational speaking circuit of survivors, like those mountaineers who cut off their own arms.

ISABEL: You do realise that is the reason women accept invitations to conferences? Simply for the pleasure of reducing their men to a state of utter fatigue-related collapse *just so they know*.

WILLIAM: Yes, actually. I did realise that. I think I rang you, *sobbing*.

Light change.

Flashback:

[*Fast*] I mixed it the way you said to. I did it just the way you said to and she started to take it and then she stopped and she wouldn't take it and then she took it. I put her in the outfit with the butterflies that Joanie gave her, the one you told me to, and I put her in the car seat but I couldn't get the strap to go in the fucking slot. It was like it was jammed, it wouldn't click, it was going in and not clicking and she was crying. I was there about twenty minutes and she was crying the whole time and finally I got it in, I was sweating like a pig, and I started the car and we were two hours late and we were just at the intersection and then she vomited. She vomited over everything, the outfit, the capsule. I'd forgotten the nappy bag anyway, so I had to go back to the house and take her in again and wipe her down and re-dress her and this time I just put her in the ugly pink towelling thing because I couldn't be fucked and then we went through the whole thing again and then we got to Alice's and you could see that Ted was pissed off I was so late *even though I'd told them not to wait*, they'd waited and then she wouldn't settle. It didn't matter what I did. She was either hungry or thirsty or tired or sick or missing you. She could be teething. She could have reflux. Ted said she's just a baby and babies do that and finally, I just gave up and decided there was no point staying for dinner if she was going to scream her head off so we came home. I was so tired I nearly ran off the road. And she screamed the entire way home like there was a pin sticking into her, this high-pitched hysterical kind of scream, it was like an insane woman's scream and it just kept going I'm surprised you didn't hear it from your fucking Scandinavian hotel suite. And then I mixed up the powdered stuff and I used the teeny-tiny spoon you told me to but she kept chucking it up and then I put her down and I'm not kidding, I kid you not, I tried the rocking, I tried the three little ducks the way you told me to, I tried Old Macdonald, I tried the Mister Whispers tape, I tried the in-utero noise tape, I tried Peter Paul and Mary, I tried silence, I tried the light on, I tried the light off, I tried elevating the mattress, I tried the night light, I tried the Babar music box, I tried 'Eensy Weensy Spider', I tried the Captain and Tenille and finally she nodded off to ACDC. So I fell into bed and I felt like I was going to die and I was just falling into that deep sleep when she woke up. She woke up and then she vomited. All over the cot and the carpet and the little chair. It's was like three square metres of regurgitated baby formula and rice cereal and so I cleaned it up with the stuff you told me to use and I wiped her down with the other stuff you told me to use and not the other stuff the one you told me not to use and then I changed her and the sheet and then I put her down and the whole thing started again and listen to me, I now know why people throw their children out of windows, they're not bad people! They're not evil people! They're just tired people*, just horribly horribly tired people* and I know it's pathetic and I know it must seem stupid but I'm so depressed and exhausted and miserable and lonely.

ISABEL: I can't *believe* you put her in the ugly pink towelling thing!

Beat.

WILLIAM: That's it?

ISABEL *laughs.*

Light change.

You laughed.

ISABEL: I laughed?

WILLIAM: From the hot tub you were sharing with some pasty art historian from some shit college in Wisconsin.

ISABEL: Oh yes… that sleek, tanned art historian from Yale… the one who read me haikus.

WILLIAM: I know you're lying because no art historian in the history of the world has ever been tanned.

ISABEL: He was the one who said, famously, that 'a beautiful woman should never be viewed under anything but candlelight'.

WILLIAM: No wonder you came home.

ISABEL: A woman hears a line like that and self control goes right out the window.

WILLIAM: *As we know.*

ISABEL: [*with longing and tenderness*] Then, she started sleeping. Everybody slept. For a year. And when we woke up, it was all good. Did we stop? For a second? Did we stand there on the street, in the park, at the supermarket? Did we ever stop, that year, and look at what we had? The three of us. For just a moment. [*Beat.*] If only you could photograph the unexceptional. Because it's so exceptional.

WILLIAM: We were, weren't we? We were happy. For a time there?

ISABEL: Yes.

WILLIAM: When I got the job?

ISABEL: Yes.

WILLIAM: I came home from the trip. You were standing in the kitchen. I walked in. With a snow dome.

Light change.

Flashback:

Now *this* is art.

ISABEL: How nice. The Hollywood sign. In snow.

WILLIAM: You can have your fucking Velázquezes.

ISABEL: I'm not sure the plural of Velázquez *is* Velázquezes. It's like sheep. Or squid. One squid, two squid.

WILLIAM: Possibly the first art conservator to compare Velázquez to calamari.

WILLIAM *starts dancing.*

ISABEL: You got it?

WILLIAM: I got it.

ISABEL: We're rich!

WILLIAM: It will get me 'noticed', as they say. Max says it's bound to make a splash. That director. And it's heart-rending.

ISABEL: Is it?

WILLIAM: It didn't render *my* heart, as a matter of fact. But who's not compelled by the tale of an eight-year-old Ecuadorian refugee in need of a heart transplant who's adopted by a dying American doctor?

ISABEL: And you are—

WILLIAM: The dying American doctor's… best friend—

ISABEL: Not the hero?

WILLIAM: Well, actually, I *am* the hero. Because I persuade the dying American doctor to adopt the Ecuadorian eight-year-old and find him a heart.

ISABEL: That's it?

WILLIAM: I end up screwing the widow.

ISABEL: In a tasteful way.

They smile.

WILLIAM: Tell me life isn't strange.

ISABEL: Max must be—

WILLIAM: *Happy*. He's a happy agent. The happiest.

They are holding each other around the waist, looking at each other.

ISABEL: Hey.

WILLIAM: Hey. [*Beat.*] Didn't I tell you I'd come good?

They kiss.

ISABEL: The second roof guy came. Three thousand *more*. Something to do with the addition. They didn't allow for something around the chimney. It has to have privets or rivets or crumpets or something. So I called the ones Ruth said were good and they're coming on Thursday. My mother rang. She's meeting up with Trevor and Elly in the Dordogne to eat at some whizz-bang place it takes four years to get into but Elly's cousin supplies them with ducks. The book arrived. The roses are out.

WILLIAM: Is she asleep?

ISABEL: Sneak in.

WILLIAM: Mention me?

ISABEL: Often. I'm making boring pasta but tomorrow we go to Adolpho's. You *star*.

Light change.

Beat.

WILLIAM: [*transfixed by the thought, but knowing*] Can I sneak in?

ISABEL: She's gone.

WILLIAM: [*with longing*] Sneak in. A single glance. A tiny glance. I won't wake her up.

ISABEL: She's gone.

WILLIAM: One look. Just a look.

ISABEL: She's gone. The room is gone.

WILLIAM: What?

ISABEL: There's an old printer in there. And a futon. Otherwise, it's bare.

WILLIAM: It's bare?

ISABEL: Yes.

WILLIAM: And her stuff?

ISABEL: Gone.

WILLIAM: All of it.

ISABEL: Every single thing.

WILLIAM: What?

ISABEL: When you didn't come. April twenty-fifth. I just—I got rid of it.

WILLIAM: [*disbelieving*] You got rid of it?

ISABEL: I waited for you. And you didn't come and something… happened.

WILLIAM: *What?*

ISABEL: Something. *Broke*. In hours, it was gone.

WILLIAM: There's nothing left?

ISABEL: Not a thing. Not a single thing. Not a nightie. Not a teddy. Photos, I've kept. A baby book with the measurements I couldn't throw away. They're in the coat cupboard. But all the rest is gone.

WILLIAM: You shouldn't have done that.

ISABEL: You didn't want them.

WILLIAM: You shouldn't have done that!

ISABEL: [*distraught*] I was the keeper of the flame. Perhaps there has to be one in every marriage. The one who stays conscious of the deeper things, pays mind to them. The other likes freedom from sentiment, memory, hates being hostage to them but needs the other to be the historian. I've been yours for five years now, William. Keeping the flame for both of us. That's enough. I'm letting her go. No more hoarding the bric-a-brac of Bea. [*Beat. Thinking as she speaks, occurring to her for the first time the argument could be put in this way*] Tell me something. If we could have lived a life without Bea at all, without her ever existing, would you have wanted that?

WILLIAM: But we can't.

ISABEL: Just pretend. For a second. Never to have known her. None of the suffering. None of the horror. But none of the happiness, either. *No Bea*. Would you choose that, William?

WILLIAM: [*deeply affected*] It's a terrible question.

ISABEL: *Would you choose never to have had her?*

The full force of ISABEL*'s argument for love is contained in this answer:*

WILLIAM: [*realising*] No.

He is devastated. Long beat.

ISABEL: [*with love*] William…

WILLIAM: Even with all of it… with all of it… No. Isabel… it was worth it.

ISABEL: Yes.

Beat.

WILLIAM: All these years… I did keep one image…

ISABEL: You did?

WILLIAM: From before Bea got sick. It was autumn and cold. I came home. Happy. I walked into the room, taking off my jacket, and looked across at you, feeding Bea in the chair.

Flashback:

WILLIAM *looks at her gravely.*

[*Suddenly, beaming*] Hello, dear ones!

ISABEL: 'Hello, dear ones,' you said. Bea broke off, arched her back, looked up at you. Her hand reached out to touch your gravelly face, smiling as if to say: *Papa*. You said:

WILLIAM: I'm opening some wine. *Fine wine*. To celebrate.

ISABEL: To celebrate what?

WILLIAM: To celebrate the moment, *this* moment.

WILLIAM *and* ISABEL *look at each other. They are on the verge of kissing, but it's ambiguous whether it's then or now. He kisses her, long, tender.*

A perfectly good moment. Better than that. [*He opens the bottle and pours the wine.*] Drink it slowly. It's not every day we have a bottle that costs eight dollars.

ISABEL: [*with love not sentiment*] *Provider.*

WILLIAM: *Madonna.* [*Beat.*] Let's go to bed early. Let's eat in bed. Let's eat takeaway in bed. Naked. And watch anything with Harrison Ford.

ISABEL: Or Jean-Claude Van Damme.

Light change.

You kissed me.

Beat.

WILLIAM: Here we are.

ISABEL: You said:

WILLIAM: Here we are. *Three.*

ISABEL: The doctor with the hair, our lovely doctor. He said: 'We'll have to operate and see what we can find'. That night, we went home to the cold house. We both of us wanted to lie alone—the first sign. But you turned to me, you took me up, you said to me:

WILLIAM: Isabel.

ISABEL: I won't forget it, what you said.

WILLIAM: We conceive children so rashly, drunk on recklessness.

ISABEL: Drunk on recklessness, you said. Yes, I said. That's the whole trick of the continuance of the species. You don't realise the terror of child-having until it's too late. We were in the waiting room. Coffee from a machine. Old women's magazines. We'd seen Bea go in. Our baby girl in a white gown, tied at the back. Who knew they made them that small?

WILLIAM: Her dear little face, astonished, looking up at us as the blue-swathed nurses wheeled her away.

Long silence, appalled, stricken, captivated by the memory.

ISABEL: Everything only *we* knew. Bea and who she was and what the world would be *minus*.

WILLIAM: Then the nurse called us.

ISABEL: I felt such pity for her. To be the bearer of such news. I started to cry for the awfulness of her job.

WILLIAM: Yes.

Beat.

ISABEL: And then... the day we were to bury her... I woke up and you were on a plane. I wanted to kill you, but only because I wanted to *be* you.

WILLIAM: Isabel—

ISABEL: It's all right.

WILLIAM: I...

ISABEL: I know.

WILLIAM: I couldn't stay.

ISABEL: I know.

WILLIAM: [*distraught*] Isabel—I—I—I couldn't say—these years—I couldn't find a way to say... But in my own way... I felt what you... I felt what you... But somewhere it could not... be spoken. And even... yes... Sometimes I *envied* you that you could turn those feelings into words. *I envied you that.* It seemed to me that no words could ever summon what... that words wouldn't do. I looked to you—somehow you found a way. Your anniversaries. The way you made containers out of days... whereas I... could only feel this jangling terror that could not be named or it would... consume me... Consume me. [*Long beat. He sobs.*] I wanted, sometimes, to pick up the phone, in the dead of night and call you and say: Help me. I'll help *you* if you help *me*. But if I started... if I started... how would I stop? Better keep it silent... keep it distant... and maybe I can just hold on, stave it off, until I disappear myself...

ISABEL *crosses to the devastated* WILLIAM *and touches him. He turns to embrace her. She holds him, as he calms his sobbing. Then she looks up, over him, to the painting. Beat.*

ISABEL: [*indicating the couple in the painting and gradually standing and moving over to it*] Look at them. Growing clearer. Slowly, the yellow varnish comes off, layer by layer. Who were they? Young, they were hopeful. They imagined something for themselves: a house, a child, a garden where the child would play. And then, what? The unruly detail of life got in their way. And did love stay? Did it persist against the odds?

ISABEL *looks across to him. They lock eyes.*

WILLIAM: There is no preparation for marriage but marriage.

ISABEL *takes the watch which has been slipped over the top of the easel and looks at it.*

ISABEL: Oh, look. Five seconds. Five. Four. Three. Two.

Blackout.

THE END

Melinda Butel as Isabel and Kim Gyngell as William in the 2008 MTC production. (Photo: Jeff Busby)

Also by Joanna Murray-Smith and available from Currency Press

Bombshells

When *Bombshells* premiered in Melbourne, the *Age* predicted that it would end up in London's West End: 'Get in quick if you want to be able to boast you were there when it all began', it advised readers. It was right. After an award-winning season in Edinburgh, *Bombshells* opened in London in September 2004. *Bombshells* exposes six women balancing their inner and outer lives with humour and often desperate cunning. They range in age from a feisty teenager to a 64-year-old widow yearning for the unexpected. Joanna Murray-Smith created these six dazzling monologues to showcase the talents of Caroline O'Connor, but they will be relished by performers everywhere.
ISBN 978 0 86819 751 7

Female of the Species

Margot Mason, celebrated feminist, academic, mother and author of bestseller *The Cerebral Vagina*, has never had any problems with inspiring adulation. As she sits in her country home, struggling with a deadline, in walks Molly Rivers, student, idealist and daughter of one of Margot's biggest fans. Initially flattered, Margot is less pleased when Molly handcuffs her to her desk and threatens to kill her. This deliciously funny farce looks at the fallout for the fans when our heroes change their mind.
ISBN 978 0 86819 825 5

Honour

After 32 years acclaimed journalist George leaves Honor, a poet, wife and mother. In the wake of his new passion for Claudia, a bright young journalist not much older than their 24-year-old daughter, Sophia, Honor must come to grips with the career she has willingly sacrificed for her husband and child, the evolution of a marriage, her abandonment and eventual resurrection. In a series of intense confrontations, the wife, husband, lover and daughter negotiate the forces of passion, lust, history, responsibility and humour. *Honour* was the winner of the 1996 Victorian Premier's Award for Drama.
ISBN 9780868197821

Love Child

A reconciliation between a mother and the daughter she gave away at birth. Anna is a successful film editor in her 40s who has defined herself through her political conscience. Living alone in a cold, stylish apartment she believes she has come to terms with her history, until a young woman called Billie arrives at her door. Billie acts in soap operas, doesn't believe in political action and wants a mother.
ISBN 978 0 86819 546 9

Nightfall

The doorbell rings. The door is opened. On the porch stands a young woman. Emily and Edward Kingsley have dreamt of this night for seven years. At the same time, however, they have shared the dread that their dream may turn into a nightmare. But nothing could have prepared them for the decision they must face which will change the nature of their relationship forever. Murray-Smith closely examines family, love and commitment with her characteristically sharp insight in this taut and compelling drama.
ISBN 978 0 86819 591 9

Rapture

A group of friends gather to celebrate the homecoming of two of their group, who went overseas after an unfortunate fire wiped out their home and possessions. When the pair arrive, however, their friends learn the truth. *Rapture* is a thoughtful and entertaining play about what happens when cynicism is confronted by faith. Winner of the Louis Esson Prize for Drama.
ISBN 978 0 86819 679 4

Switzerland

It's 1995 in the Swiss Alps and the ailing reclusive crime writer Patricia Highsmith is visited by a genial young man from her New York publisher, sent to convince her to write the final instalment of her best-selling *Mr Ripley* series. What first appears to be a standard cat-and-mouse game of wit and wiles soon becomes a dance to the death. Who is the cat and who is the mouse? And who will make it out of Switzerland alive? A chilling and sometimes hilarious two-hander, with Murray-Smith's signature lucid-lettered prose.
ISBN 978-1-92500-556-1, also available as an ebook